REMEMBER *the* LADIES!

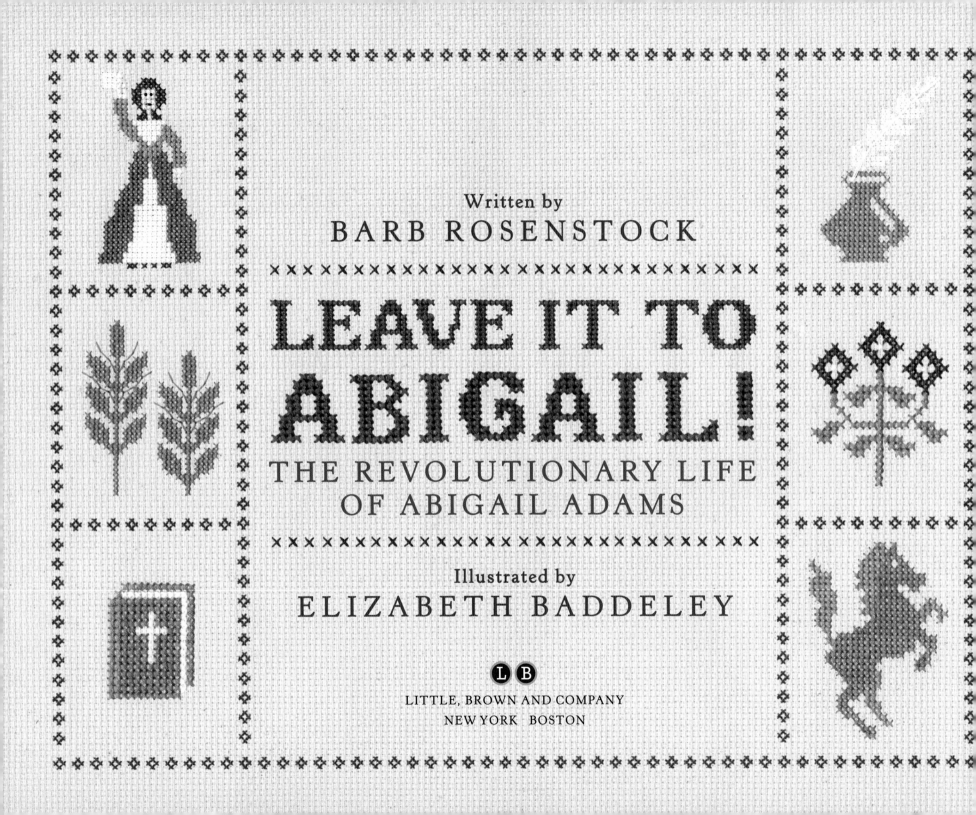

Written by

BARB ROSENSTOCK

LEAVE IT TO ABIGAIL!

THE REVOLUTIONARY LIFE
OF ABIGAIL ADAMS

Illustrated by

ELIZABETH BADDELEY

LB

LITTLE, BROWN AND COMPANY

NEW YORK   BOSTON

I N A CLAPBOARD HOUSE
in the colony of Massachusetts,
a baby girl's weak cries drowned
in the cold November wind.
Her worried parents hurried to
bless and name her. But Abigail
surprised everyone—she lived.

Abigail grew up in a time when
most colonial girls learned just
enough words to read the Bible and
just enough math to shop.

Everyone knew that good girls
kept quiet, but . . .

LEAVE IT TO ABIGAIL...

She ignored Mother's chores and explored Father's books.

She blurted out questions and eavesdropped on visitors.

She bossed her sisters, brother, and anyone else who would listen.

Only Grandmother Quincy understood:

"Wild colts make the best horses."

Little by little, Abigail tamed herself. She finished tasks before reading. She learned to milk, bake, stew, salt, card, spin, knit, and weave. Abigail banked fires, raised chicks, and brewed herb medicines. Everyone knew she should marry a prosperous minister.

LEAVE IT TO ABIGAIL...

She met a struggling country lawyer named John Adams.

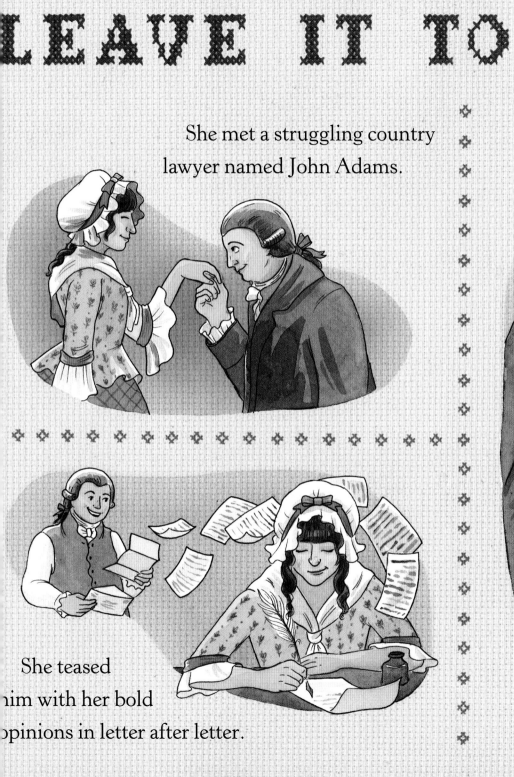

She teased him with her bold opinions in letter after letter.

She insisted on marrying the man she loved.

Abigail stitched shirts, dipped candles, and rocked their babies while John ran their farm and practiced law from the house. She reviewed John's notes on cases and clients.

Soon he opened a second office ten miles away in Boston. Abigail
packed up the family and moved with John, farm to city, city to farm,
and back again.

Out her city window, Abigail saw Boston marching toward rebellion. England's King George forced American colonists to pay taxes on everyday items: first sugar, then tea, glass, paints, even paper! But colonists had no say in how their taxes were spent by England's government. People boycotted. Leaders organized.

The king blocked Boston Harbor, sent soldiers and ships to keep the colonies quiet. Riots broke out. People died.

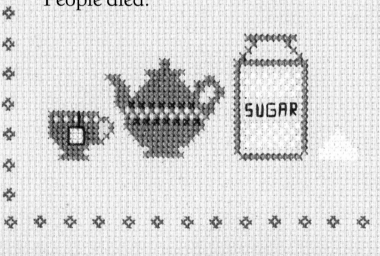

John wrote articles supporting colonial rights. Abigail shaped John's words and shared her opinions. The colonies' leaders decided to meet. Would they fight for independence? John left for this Continental Congress in Philadelphia—three hundred miles away. Everyone knew that a woman couldn't manage a farm alone.

LEAVE IT TO ABIGAIL...

She dug potatoes and hired farmhands to mend fences and harvest hay.

She preserved food and taught all four children.

She fed the militia and housed refugees fleeing Boston as the war for independence spread.

Across Massachusetts Bay, the British cannons roared. Abigail turned worries into words. She wrote to family, friends, and always to John. He called her reports about troop movements and supplies "clearer and fuller Intelligence, than I can get from a whole Committee of Gentlemen."

Abigail wrote about women, too. She knew America's revolution depended on wives, mothers, and daughters. Without them—no meals, uniforms, or blankets.

Women raised money, hauled water, and nursed injured soldiers. They
spied. Some fought. Just before the Declaration of Independence was signed,

Abigail wrote John her boldest letter yet: America's women deserved rights, too!
John thought she must be joking. Abigail was not amused.

The tiny American army lost battle after battle. Congress sent John to France to ask its king for help. He took their oldest son along but left Abigail at home with the other children. Everyone knew that a mother couldn't support a whole family!

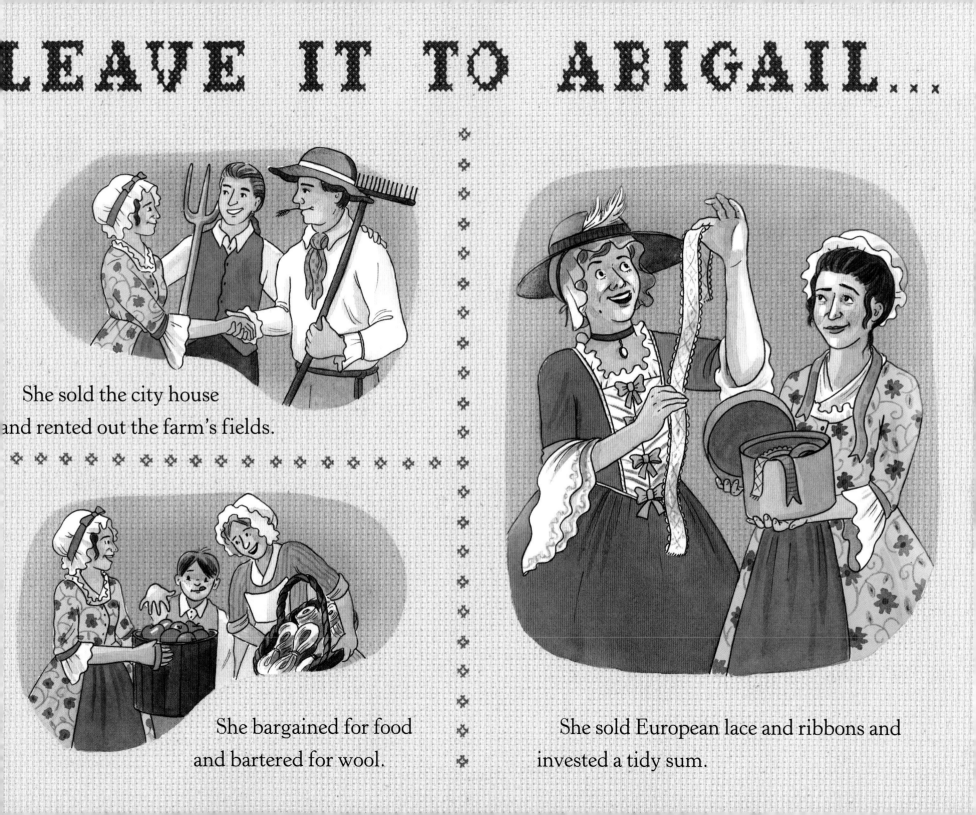

LEAVE IT TO ABIGAIL...

She sold the city house
and rented out the farm's fields.

She bargained for food
and bartered for wool.

She sold European lace and ribbons and
invested a tidy sum.

Abigail managed money, used words, and understood people
better than John. She loved politics just as much.

She wrote congressmen, dined on the French admiral's ship,
and met George Washington, John Hancock, and Ben Franklin.

Abigail and John lived thousands of miles apart when America won its freedom. With their children almost grown, she longed to meet him in Europe. Everyone knew that ladies didn't belong at sea!

LEAVE IT TO ABIGAIL...

She boarded a filthy schooner, threw up for ten days, then charmed the captain.

She ordered the ship scrubbed from gangplank to galley, unpacked her own dishes, and whipped up tasty puddings!

She survived wild storms, watched the night waves glow, and memorized the sails' names.

Still, after thirty days at sea, she'd never been so bored in her life....

It was all worth it to be together. Abigail lived with John in France and England while he served as ambassador for the new United States. John and Abigail didn't have enough money to impress the fancy Europeans. Everyone knew the Americans would embarrass their young country.

LEAVE IT TO ABIGAIL...

She furnished a thirty-room mansion, supervised servants, and hosted diplomatic dinners—on less than $20 a day.

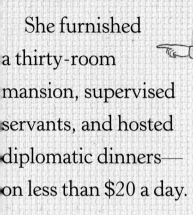

She shopped the latest fashions and mingled at glittering concerts.

She stuck a feathered cap on her head, crammed her bustle into a gilt carriage, and chatted with kings and queens.

Four years later, Abigail and John returned home to cheering crowds.
John Adams became the vice president under President George Washington.
Later, he was elected the second president of the United States. Everyone
knew that the president's *wife* should stay out of politics!

LEAVE IT TO ABIGAIL...

She threw parties for politicians, greeted thousands of visitors, and briefed John on political gossip.

She discussed appointments, edited speeches, and researched foreign affairs, serving as the president's most important advisor.

Reporters nicknamed her "Mrs. President." In rooms full of influential men, Abigail held the most power. When people wanted a government job or an idea passed on to President Adams, they wrote to Abigail first.

When their time in Washington ended, John and Abigail retired from politics to a large farm they called Peacefield. Grandchildren romped about the house, and the letters never stopped flying. Family, friends, servants, and politicians relied on Abigail's wise advice until her last days. Everyone knew there'd never be another woman like her…

PATSY TAKEMOTO MINK

CORETTA SCOTT KING

DOLORES HUERTA

She left the hope of freedom to America's women—
daughters, wives, mothers,
thinkers, writers, revolutionaries—

girls who surprised the world.

GLORIA STEINEM

HILLARY CLINTON

WINONA LADUKE

AUTHOR'S NOTE

At a time when women couldn't own property, sign contracts, or earn money directly, Abigail Adams spent more than two decades managing a family, farm, and finances while her husband, John, helped run a revolution. He could not have survived without her. Yet her crucial contributions to the beginning of our country have often been minimized or ignored.

Abigail Smith was born on November 11, 1744. She was not sent to school. Instead, she read her way through her father's library and learned from conversations with educated visitors. By the time she met John Adams, she was a bright fourteen-year-old who wasn't afraid to speak her mind. John thought she was entirely too outspoken. But they soon fell in love, and married when John was twenty-four and Abigail was nineteen.

Abigail and John lived apart for years at a time, missed each other constantly, and wrote each other often. They also wrote family, friends, and business partners. John was an accomplished legal writer, but Abigail's personality shines through her words. She didn't always spell or use punctuation properly, yet her exceptional writing *voice* communicates her intense feelings about the times in which she lived. No one of her time wrote more naturally, and no one better proved the capabilities of women.

But that does not mean Abigail Adams thought women were equal in the modern sense. She believed, as did most everyone of her time, that men were in charge of the outside world, while women should be obedient wives and mothers. Her legacy as one of America's earliest women's rights advocates comes from her March 31, 1776 letter to John in which she expressed her opinion about women's rights under the law:

> *I long to hear that you have declared an independancy—and by the way in the new Code of Laws which I suppose it will be necessary for you to make I desire you would* **Remember the Ladies***, and be more generous and favourable to them than your ancestors.*

John's response was typical of men of his time: "I cannot but laugh."

Abigail also felt that African Americans deserved more legal protection. She grew up with at least two slaves, Tom and Phoebe, in her father's home. Tom's life story is lost to history, but Phoebe chose emancipation when Abigail's father died. As a free woman, she worked for pay in the Adams household as a trusted caretaker of their home. Abigail and John never owned slaves; they both wrote consistently about slavery's many evils and could not understand how other founders of the United States reconciled slaveholding with beliefs about human rights.

There is much to admire in a woman who was born in a tiny colonial home, milked cows, pulled weeds, met royalty, and became the first First Lady to live in the White House. But the most impressive thing about Abigail Adams is that she learned so much on her own through reading, talking to others, and writing. In one of her last letters, before she died at the age of seventy-three, she writes about family, weather, politics, art, and a book of female biographies that she "should like to read." I hope she did.

In trying to represent Abigail's living spirit, I sorted through hundreds of biographies of American women who carried on her independent legacy. The twelve women I chose for the final pages of the story were indeed thinkers, writers, and revolutionaries like Abigail. But the choices are not exclusive. My original list ran to four single-spaced pages including such accomplished women as Lucretia Mott, Harriet Tubman, Lucy Burns, Grace Lee Boggs, Emma Tenayuca, Betty Friedan, Marilyn French, Shirley Chisholm, Gloria Anzaldúa, Angela Davis, Mazie Hirono, Sylvia Rivera, and Linda Sarsour, some of whom are still working today. With the help of experts, I focused on women from different eras whose accomplishments have stood the test of time.

My thanks to Sara Georgini, series editor, papers of John Adams, at the Massachusetts Historical Society; Caroline Keinath, deputy superintendent at the Adams National Historical Park; and Cathy Torrey, of the Abigail Adams Birthplace, for sharing their knowledge of Abigail's life. This book is dedicated to Riley, Lexi, Hannah, Olivia, Emily, and all the young women who will change the world.

ARTIST'S NOTE

I work in a number of mediums, including pen, ink, watercolor, and colored pencil. This is the first book I partially illustrated with needle and thread, though! Cross-stitch is a form of embroidery where X-shaped stitches are grouped together to create words and images. Cross-stitch samplers were a popular pastime for young girls growing up in colonial America. In addition to teaching them the important skill of sewing, samplers were intended to help girls learn the alphabet, numbers, and even Bible verses. This art form has also long been a part of my personal story. My mom, to whom I dedicated this book, taught me how to cross-stitch when I was about the age of young Abigail running in the field with the animals!

Abigail Adams was a woman of many talents and responsibilities. The challenge for me as an illustrator was how to depict her multitude of skills in a way that is easy for readers to digest. I came up with the idea of using a cross-stitch sampler to organize the many facets of Abigail Adams's life, while still staying true to the era in which she lived. I also decided to juxtapose colorful, sometimes patterned clothing and settings with the muted, more formal cross-stitch to call attention to Abigail's nonconformity and to visually allude to the many ways that she was well ahead of her time.

SELECTED SOURCES

- *Adams Family Papers: An Electronic Archive*. Massachusetts Historical Society, masshist.org/digitaladams.
- Gelles, Edith (ed.). *Abigail Adams, Letters*. New York: Library of America, 2016.
- Gelles, Edith B. *Portia—The World of Abigail Adams*. Bloomington: Indiana University Press, 1992.
- Holton, Woody. *Abigail Adams*. New York: Free Press, 2009.
- Levin, Phyllis Lee. *Abigail Adams—A Biography*. New York: Thomas Dunne Books, (1987) 2002.
- Withey, Lynne. *Dearest Friend—A Life of Abigail Adams*. New York: Touchstone, (1981) 2002.

- "Wild colts..." Abigail Adams to John Quincy Adams, December 30, 1804, founders.archives.gov/documents/Adams/99-03-02-1372
- "Clearer and fuller..." John Adams to Mary Palmer, Philadelphia, July 5, 1776, masshist.org/publications/adams-papers/index.php/view/ADMS-04-02-02-0018#sn=0
- "I long to..." Abigail Adams to John Adams, March 31, 1776, masshist.org/publications/adams-papers/index.php/view/ADMS-04-01-02-0241#sn=0
- "I cannot but..." John Adams to Abigail Adams, April 14, 1776, masshist.org/publications/adams-papers/index.php/view/ADMS-04-01-02-0248#sn=52
- "Should like to..." Abigail Adams to Caroline Smith De Windt, March 22, 1818. Gelles (*Letters*), p. 952–53.

ABOUT THIS BOOK

This book was edited by Deirdre Jones and designed by Jen Keenan and Saho Fujii. The production was supervised by Erika Breglia, and the production editor was Annie McDonnell. The text was set in Horley Old Style MT, and the display type was hand-lettered.

ABIGAIL
ADAMS